T0414180

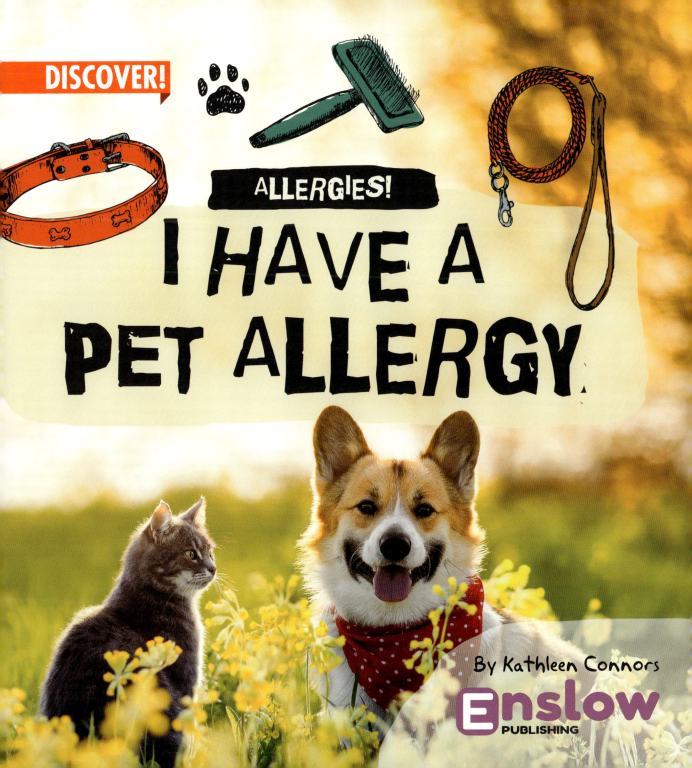

DISCOVER!

ALLERGIES!

I HAVE A PET ALLERGY

By Kathleen Connors

Enslow
PUBLISHING

Please visit our website, www.enslow.com. For a free color catalog of all our high-quality books, call toll free 1-800-398-2504 or fax 1-877-980-4454.

Library of Congress Cataloging-in-Publication Data

Names: Connors, Kathleen, author.
Title: I have a pet allergy / Kathleen Connors.
Description: Buffalo, New York : Enslow Publishing, [2024] | Series:
    Allergies! | Includes index. | Audience: Grades K-1
Identifiers: LCCN 2022045228 (print) | LCCN 2022045229 (ebook) | ISBN
    9781978533844 (library binding) | ISBN 9781978533837 (paperback) | ISBN
    9781978533851 (ebook)
Subjects: LCSH: Allergy in children–Juvenile literature.
Classification: LCC RJ386 .C66 2024 (print) | LCC RJ386 (ebook) | DDC
    618.92/97–dc23/eng/20220923
LC record available at https://lccn.loc.gov/2022045228
LC ebook record available at https://lccn.loc.gov/2022045229

Portions of this work were originally authored by Maria Nelson and published as *I'm Allergic to Pets*. All new material this edition authored by Kathleen Connors.

Published in 2024 by
Enslow Publishing
2544 Clinton Street
Buffalo, NY 14224

Copyright © 2024 Enslow Publishing

Designer: Claire Wrazin
Editor: Kristen Nelson

Photo credits: Cover (photo) Bachkova Natalia/Shutterstock.com; Cover (art), pp. 2, 6, 10, 16, 22 Milanana/Shutterstock.com; Cover (art, paw print), pp. 4, 14 Mureu/Shutterstock.com; Series Art (texture) arigato/Shutterstock.com; p. 5 Sunflower Light Pro/Shutterstock.com; p. 7 Anatta_Tan/Shutterstock.com; p. 9 Tatyana Soares/Shutterstock.com; p. 11 Prostock-studio/Shutterstock.com; p. 13 JPC-PROD/Shutterstock.com; p. 15 Microgen/Shutterstock.com; p. 17 Yuliya Evstratenko/Shutterstock.com; p. 19 Dmytro Vietrov/Shutterstock.com; p. 21 Elena Sherengovskaya/Shutterstock.com

Printed in the United States of America

Some of the images in this book illustrate individuals who are models. The depictions do not imply actual situations or events.

CPSIA compliance information: Batch #CS24ENS: For further information contact Enslow Publishing, at 1-800-398-2504.

Find us on

CONTENTS

Boldface words appear in Words to Know.

RUNS IN THE FAMILY

Did you know you're more likely to have pet allergies if a parent does? It's true! Allergies are caused by your body **reacting** badly to matter that's commonly safe for most people.

People aren't born with pet allergies.
They develop over time.

5

WHAT'S THE CAUSE?

Animal saliva, or drool, can cause allergic reactions. So can **urine**. Most often, though, animals' skin **cells**, called dander, are the problem. Dander, saliva, and urine all have a **protein** in them that can cause an allergic reaction.

6

Dogs, cats, and horses are some of the most common pets people are allergic to.

Pet dander is so tiny you can't see it! It stays in the air a long time. Dander spreads around the house because animals shed, or lose, their fur and hair. It sticks to your clothes and furniture. It's very hard to get rid of.

Pet birds have dander too!

ACHOO!

Allergic reactions to pets commonly happen soon after a person is around pets. Pet allergies can seem a lot like a cold. People with pet allergies sneeze, cough, and get watery eyes. Their nose, mouth, and throat might start to feel itchy.

10

Visiting a house with pets can be hard for those with allergies.

11

For someone with asthma, pet allergies will often be worse. They'll have a hard time breathing. Whether or not you have asthma, if allergic reactions get worse or last for a long time, it's time to see a doctor.

Asthma is an illness that affects the lungs. A person's airways become narrower at times, making it hard to breathe.

WHICH ANIMAL?

Sometimes a person is most allergic to cats, for example. Other times, a person is allergic to many pets. A skin **prick** test shows what's causing your allergies. A small amount of an **allergen** is placed under your skin to see if a reaction occurs.

A special doctor called an allergist will give a skin prick test.

15

ALLERGY MANAGEMENT

One way to manage pet allergies is with **medicine**. You can also bathe pets often to cut down on dander. Give the person who has allergies at least one room that pets aren't allowed in, such as their bedroom.

16

People with pet allergies should try not to hug or kiss pets too.

Cleaning your home well can help with allergies. But, it takes months for your house to be allergen-free. You likely won't feel better right away. Staying away from pets is the only sure way you'll have fewer allergic reactions.

Using special kinds of dust cloths and vacuums can help keep dander down in your home.

NEW PET?

If you or a family member have bad allergic reactions, you can still have a pet! Certain kinds of pets are less likely to cause allergic reactions. A lizard or fish could be the right pet for you!

There are lots of animals out there to love!

WORDS TO KNOW

allergen: Matter that causes an allergy.

cell: The smallest basic part of a living thing.

develop: To happen over time.

medicine: A drug used to make a sick person well.

prick: To break the skin with a sharp point.

protein: A necessary element found in all living things.

react: To respond.

urine: A yellow liquid containing water and waste products that flows out of an animal's body.

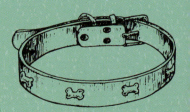

FOR MORE INFORMATION

BOOKS

Brundle, Joanna. *Asthma and Allergies*. New York, NY: KidHaven Publishing, an imprint of Greenhaven Publishing, 2022.

Duhig, Holly. *Understanding Allergies*. New York, NY: PowerKids Press, 2019.

WEBSITES

All About Allergies

kidshealth.org/parent/medical/allergies/allergy.html#
Find out how to live with many different kinds of allergies.

Just for Kids: Allergy and Asthma Games, Puzzles

www.aaaai.org/conditions-treatments/just-for-kids
Find fun ways to understand allergies and asthma better on this site for kids.

INDEX